To
Amy
Millie
Holly
Sophia

"The future belongs to those who believe in the beauty of their dreams."

(Eleanor Roosevelt)

What's In This Book?

Chapter 1
The Normal Person
4

Chapter 2
Mental Health Is Real
9

Chapter 3
The Normal 'Work' Day
17

Chapter 4
Should You Get A Tattoo?
27

Chapter 5
Is It Normal To Be Lonely?
34

Chapter 6
Do You Need To Drive?
44

Chapter 7
Should You Have Children?
51

Chapter 8
Want A Mortgage?
56

Chapter 9
We're All Going On A Summer Holiday
61

Chapter 10
My Family Support
66

Chapter 11
Should We All Exercise?
72

Chapter 12
Be Connected, It's Normal?
79

Chapter 13
Are We Overwhelmed?
83

Chapter 14
Addiction Is Simply Normality?
87

Chapter 15
What's Normality?
93

Chapter 1
The Normal Person

If you've read my first book, "Living With Aspergers: Daniel's Story" you'll already know a lot about me. In fact, you'll know:

I have Asperger's or you can call it, autism.
I've been through a psychotic episode.
I struggle every day to be seen as "normal".

The question I want to ask though is, "What's Normality?".
I want to delve deeper into the question and expose the so called "normal" person we promote in today's capitalist society. To put this into context, from my autistic eyes and my basic view of society, today's normal person has a:

- A job
- A house
- Children
- A car
- Is married
- Can drive
- Has a degree
- Has money
- Can use a smartphone
- Can hold a conversation
- Has friends
- No tattoos
- Is independent
- Is HAPPY?

Reading the list above of normality factors may be quite hard hitting to see. Isn't this what we're told though? The normal person you see on television is what's expected of us in today's world.

What does a 'normal' person look like?

I've realised that the representation of the 'typical persan' is pure judgement. Most people do not confirm to the standard of society. I see this day in, day out, if you have a disability like autism, ADHD or a mental illness, it's so hard to confirm to the normal standard of society. So many people get obsessed with this idea of being "normal", whatever this maybe. Maybe we need to take a step back and investigate what makes us HAPPY instead? Sally Rooney's book "Normal People" reflects on the idea that we construct the perfect human being. We spend our lives wanting to be, as Rooney calls it a "constructed individual".

In this book, I want to look closer at the way our society portrays normality worldwide. I want to explore how us Aspies are seen as "different". I'm going to talk to fellow people with Asperger's and get their perception into what they think is "normal". Just what is a "normal" person? Is it okay to have a face full of tattoos? Is it okay to rent a property instead of buying one? Is it okay to stay silent during a group conversation? Is it okay to just listen during a conversation?

Think about what makes YOU happy

Having autism makes it incredibly difficult to confirm with normality. Aspies across the world face ever increasing anxiety to be as 'normal' as they can be. I recently finished reading a book called 'Calm' by ex-radio DJ, Fearne Cotton. She suffers with her mental health, so she knows what it's like to be different. She explores how we're constantly under threat to be seen as the perfect fit. She explores how it's so difficult to live in a world that demands so much pressure on us. We constantly want the latest gadget, the latest trend or fashion item. I'm guilty of this because I'm always after the latest thing. For example at Xmas, I got a huge 4,000-piece Lego set which creates the Harry Potter bank, Gringotts. It looks amazing and even has the vault they go down in to get the gold. Plus, I recently bought a robotic hoover, we called it Honey. The app you use to control the hoover is called Honey.

Although having the latest gadgets can be a good thing, it can also be a negative. I recently noticed how my smart watch was giving me constant mobile notifications. This caused me extreme anxiety as I was constantly checking my watch. Today, I have a basic watch. A watch that can tell the time and nothing else. I'm finally free from the constant battle of mobile notifications. These so-called notifications get in the way of daily life, you're constantly checking what that notification is, time and time again. It's not just mobile notifications, adverts are everywhere on social media, making it almost impossible to be attracted to the latest thing.

To start examining the complexities of 'normality', I took the word 'normal' and broke its definition down. The Oxford English Dictionary defines the word 'normal' as:

'Confirming to a standard; usual, typical, or expected'

Let's start there shall we, it's obvious the word "normal" puts a lot of pressure on people. That's why this book is not going to be like any other book. It's going to explore the 'difference' we promote today rather than accepting normality. Why do we have to live the ideal life? Why can't it come with a difference? Why don we have to confirm to the normality of society?

Recently I watched an interesting sitcom exploring the world of "difference". It was called "Changing Ends" and told the comedian, Alan Carr's childhood story.

Alan lived in Northampton and was gay, played football but didn't enjoy it. Alan was a pretty standard geek and didn't really fit in. People treated Alan as different because he spoke with a high voice. He also portrayed a very different style of body langauge to everyone else. In the first episode, Alan's Mum tries to organise him a party,

so he could fit in? The thing is, why does this so called 'Alan' have to fit in? Why can't society just accept the way he is? The end of the episode sees Alan play football resulting in him kicking a ball at a fan's head.

I was bullied every single day at school

It''s obvious that people are 'different' nowadays, there's nothing wrong with that. If you look at autistic people, we may be quiet during social situations but inside we're the same. Looking closer at the LGBTQ+ community, there's constantly a battle going on around the world to be equal. I don't have anything bad to say about LGBTQ+, at the end of the day we are all human. We all have the right to be seen as different.

We are all equal

In fact, I just applied for a job promoting inclusion and diversity. Would you believe there are actually companies that have this expetise? They're called Purple Goat and have worked with major brands including Google and Currys. It's painful to see that we need companies like Purple Goat to raise awarerness of disability. I see autism as an amazing talent, why don't we embrace more of it? For example, I'm an exceptionally good writer, hence this book is full of such interesting detail. I hope it is anyway.

Chapter 2
Mental Health Is Real

It's okay, not to be okay

Ever been sectioned in a mental health ward? A lot of humans tend to think there's something wrong with you, if you suffer from mental health. It's wrong, you shouldn't be labelled mentally ill for the rest of your life. Of course, you are prone to re-lapse but after a while you're okay, in fact you're stronger. Sometimes I feel there's a label being put on me. The label that I'm psychotic all the time but of course I'm not. I've made a full recovery and I'm pleased to say that I'm very stable. I'm even off my anti-psychotic medication.

I'm hesitant to write about my psychotic episode, I always have been. I'm nervous of the way people perceive me. When i meet people, I really want to tell them about my journey. I feel I have to so careful but I am getting more confident in talking about it. In terms of employment, employers often think that I'm not capable of doing a job simply because of my mental health. This is the complete wrong way of looking at things. For example, I must be clever or else how have I written this book? I want this book to reach as many people as possible. I want to share how being mentally ill is completely a normal thing, that could happen to anybody not just a few.

I'm hesitant to write about my psychotic episode

I'm hoping this book will get across that mental health is completely normal. That's why this chapter is called "mental health is normal". If you've been in a mental health ward, you'll tend to be perceived as someone who could cause great harm. Now we all know this is not true, many people facing mental health are very clever. They have a great talent, but they simply faced a breakdown within their brain.

I've found various articles promoting the positive side of mental health. A quick Google search for "psych ward" revealed a series of articles raising awareness of mental health. The first article I come across was about a new garden facility being opened by the owner of Oldham Athletic. The garden was going to be in a mental health unit. Another article was about the tennis player, Nick Kyrgios. Nick openly admitted being sent to hospital after losing the Wimbledon final.

Mental health can impact anyone no matter how they seem

Norwich Football Club also posted a video showing two fans sat in a stadium. One of the fans was cheering, whilst the other fan just sat there with his hand on his chin. Until one day, the talkative fan doesn't turn up. It's assumed the happy, talkative man died. It's a powerful video and demonstrates how mental health can impact anyone, no matter how they seem. Have a friend to chat with? Ask if they are okay today.

When I had my psychotic episode, I was the last person I thought mental health would impact. I was running, going to the gym, working full time with lovely people. Then suddenly, BAM. I started seeing clowns. I started hearing voices which were talking to me over a period of a month. These voices become more and more prominent in my everyday life.

I was the last person I thought mental health would impact

Labelling people with mental health is a problem. A report in Psychology Today found that 20% of adults will suffer with a mental health condition.

It then went on to explain how we can eradicate the stigma of labelling patients with mental health.

The first pointer the article suggests is to make mental health a dinner table topic. Don't be scared to talk about mental health and how you're feeling, especially if it's with family or friends.

Make mental health a dinner table topic

Me and my family laugh about the times I was psychotic. We talk about it openly. I think being open is the key, being open and chatting about your problems rather than hiding them away.

I worry for the children of today when it comes to anxiety. Anxiety is reaching boiling point; we as humans are becoming constantly afraid to do things. When I was younger, I was afraid to go into a shop, but I challenged myself and did it. I think accepting you have anxiety is key to excelling. If you don't accept it then you can't challenge it. For example, many people stay within their comfort zone and don't focus on expanding it. Being comfortable only makes it more and more harder when you want to break out of it. I urge adults and children to do something different each day, then you'll be on the road to success.

It's so important to be born with a growth mindset, especially if you have autism or mental health. I think many autistics have this mindset built into them because we're always challenging ourselves to do more. Our brain isn't wired to deal with social situations, so we're constantly having to think outside the box. Some autistic people choose to wear headphones to block out the noise in a busy pub. Others write down notes to use during conversations. Some autistic people are good at acting because they can be a completely different person.

Anyway, back to the point I was making about mental health and its perception in society. I feel this book is a chance for me to explore my psychotic episode. What do people really feel when they become psychotic? I thoroughly believe that the feelings I felt when I was psychotic meant something. They shouldn't just be trashed, just because they don't confirm to the standards of society.

The psychotic feelings I felt meant something, they still mean something today

When I first got ill, I started seeing clowns. Now when I say I was seeing clowns, I I mean they were hallucinations of killer clowns. I I remember going on a walk and all I could see in the woods were killer clowns. There was even one clown waving to me from inside my village cafe. Why did I see clowns though? The brain is such a complex thing, it remembered that I was scared of clowns when I was younger.

My nan used to dress up as clowns at the local village fete and I used to run away. I'm not scared of clowns anymore. In fact, just before I got ill I went and saw IT 2, the Stephen King movie. I would go and see the movie again if I wanted too. The film wouldn't trigger me because as an adult, I know what I went though and understand the reasoning behind it.

Moving away from clowns, I also heard voices, telling me to do horrible things. These voices were supposed to be my inner voice telling me to harm my Mum, Dad and my family.

It was a scary time for me as I didn't know what was going on. Gradually these voices in my head became more prominent. My brain started following these voices as they became my version of normality. One example of this was when I tried to stab my Dad. I thought I was in a play. The police, who I thought were also actors, had to pin me down on the sofa. Then I was thankfully taken away to a mental health hospital where I made a full recovery in 6 weeks. I wasn't aware I was in hospital, in fact I remained psychotic for several weeks.

I heard these voices because I thought they were my brain; I thought my brain was talking to me. I now know the warning signs to look out for, should it happen again. I also did a course with the Early Interventions Service to understand the signs to look for, should a re-lapse occur.

To tell you the truth, I can't believe I'm off my anti-psychotics. I used to look down on people who took tablets because I used to be so

14

against taking tablets. I mean, tablets saved my life. If it wasn't for the scientists who developed my anti-psychotic, I wouldn't be here today. I'd like to thank the researchers, the scientists who worked tirelessly to create a tablet that can change someone's thinking.

What I want to understand though is, how I can go through an episode and still remember everything? It's amazing how the brain works, to go through something like that and then think how stupid you looked. All the thoughts and feelings I felt were completely rational within my brain at the time. For example, I thought I had x-ray vision, that I could read into newspapers and see who started covid. It sounds stupid, but the thing is, my brain was telling me it was true, so I believed it.

A great example of how this can happen to you is through the media, if the media tell you that broccoli causes cancer you would believe them. If they told you cauliflower makes you have better eyesight you would believe them. Until eventually you'd believe everything they'd

say. They could make up anything they like, just to control the way you think. This is exactly how my psychotic episode developed,. I was constantly being told messages and I believed them. Not just that, it was a turbulent time in the world, coronavirus had struck, the world was collapsing. Nobody could predict what was going to happen in the world, so my brain couldn't cope and went psychotic.

The 2020 pandemic changed everything

wwNow if you're reading this in the year 2103, you probably won't know what coronavirus was. It was a 'deadly' disease that struck and we all had to wear masks. Shops, hairdressers, pubs as well as huge events were all cancelled. Basically, it was a version of the apocalypse except the illness people caught didn't turn them into zombies. Nothing was normal back when coronavirus struck in 2020, everything changed. It was a turbulent time for everyone and sadly my brain went along with it.

I initially started feeling ill when I began working from home. My anxiety increased, I started feeling different within myself. I really didn't expect to be sat here writing a book about my psychosis. I thought I'd be in work, leading a team with a major social media project.
It doesn't matter though as life can change.

Just because I'm working doesn't mean I'll be happy. I went to a mental health event where I live. There was a man there who kindly opened up about his experiences. The man was Head of Wimbledon events and worked on some major events. The thing is, this man wasn't happy, he suffered from depression, so he left his job. I'm glad to say he's happy now and in a much smaller position. Mental health can impact anyone, there's evidence in so many stories. It's becoming the norm, ever since the covid epidemic.

**Dear person reading this
The world is a better place
with you in it.
Lots of love
The person in front of you
X**

Chapter 3
The Normal 'Work' Day

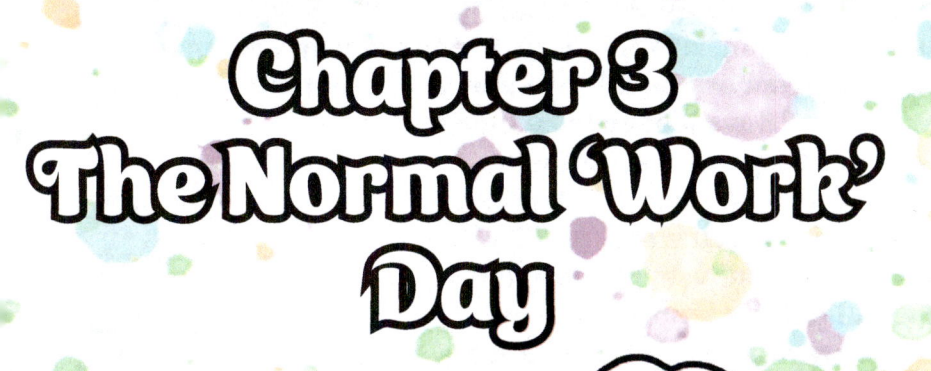

It kills me every day, the normality of having a job, a career, a way of "paying into" society. Think about it, do humans really need a work position to survive? What even is 'work' anyway and does it need to be paid? Is it necessary to get up at 6am, drive for an hour, then sit at a desk for 8 hours? If you work, you'll often have dinner really, really late too, especially if you have to commute. It's such a miserable life and often feels like you're being controlled by some kind of dictator.

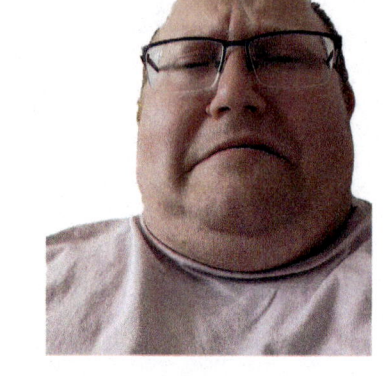

In this chapter, I want to delve deeper into the norm of the working day person. I want to explore whether the stereotypical approach of working 9am to 5pm and living a "normal life" has now broken or even disappeared.

Has the working pattern of life changed?

What do I mean by a "normal" life though? As I said at the start of this book, the media construct life. We're expected to own a house, have children, a job and more. Most people I know don't have that, it's a constructed image. I write in my blog that it's all about mindset, most of us are being told that we should go to work. Then come home to very little 'me' time. This is the mindset that's pumped into us from a very young age.

However, the mindset we should be aiming for is a HAPPY mindset. A balance between a good time and work time. I want to be able to go on holiday, to the theatre, bowling, cinema, but do I really need to work for so long? If you think about it, it's like torture, being sat in an office or on

the shop floor, being told you have to do these hours. I'm not saying I've never enjoyed working, I have. I enjoyed talking to colleagues, it's the driving,
I really didn't enjoy.

Combining 'work' and 'me' time is crucial. I feel more people will be working part time, especially if they have a family. Modern life takes its toll, more and more people are suffering from mental health. In fact, the Microsoft Work Trend Report found the 9am to 5pm trend is slowly disappearing,

DANIEL JONES

Having autism makes it extremely hard for me to find work. I've often applied for hundreds of jobs, been invited to interview but fail at that stage. My CV is superb, I know how to sell myself visually, with words and graphics. Hence why I'm looking for a role in social media but the problem arises when I attend an interview.

A **fully rounded**, **hardworking**, **ambitious** individual...

At the interview stage, I struggle to find the words I'm looking for, similar to when I'm in a social environment. This makes me look unprepared, it makes me look as if I struggle to communicate and wouldn't fit in. From an employers perspective, this is so judgemental, what if that person is generally shy, nervous, scared or fearful? I really think the days of intense interviews have gone. Companies should give you a chance to excel yourself by offering you a job specific test or a day's work to prove your skills. Yes of course, a casual chat is fine but not an interview where you're constantly being blasted with questions and being put under pres

Hello Mr Jones

Continous interview questions are likely to increase the candidate's anxiety and make them appear useless. The thing to remember here is that we are all "human". We all behave in different ways, some of us are good talkers, some of us are good listeners. We all have different traits, we all should be given a chance of expressing ourselves. In other words, the human species is not "normal", we behave in different ways.

To be honest, my career path since I've been born has been pretty positive, it's now 2024 and I've excelled in most things like working for 7 years at VTUK, working at Top Kids Accessories and Canonbury Healthcare.

So, What's Normal?

Before university in 2019, I didn't need to earn money as I was at college doing A-Levels in media studies, drama and history, I saved over £1,000 just from my paper round, so I had plenty of savings to live with. I did do some cleaning at a local pub in my village. I hoovered, mopped, dusted, empty the bins and cleaned the toilets. It only used to take me an hour and then I used to be finished. I've also worked at Sainsburys during the Christmas period. I didn't enjoy Sainsbury's when the customers came up to ask you questions about where a product was, but I did it.

After university, I started looking into my career much closer. That being marketing and social media. I literally just applied for thousands of jobs, I had an online system I could record all my applications on, which also acted as a reference for my job seekers allowance. I went to interview after interview before I was eventually offered two positions. One was a part time position with Micro Rainbow International whilst the other was full time at VTUK. I knew travelling to VTUK would be difficult for me to begin with. I started early which was good as it meant I could arrive at the office whilst there was plenty of parking.

I enjoyed my time at VTUK, my colleagues were very friendly and easy to talk too, I remember a chap called Dave, he used to always joke with me. Dave used to always ask me why I'm always on social media, I knew he was joking as it was my job. My boss was a chap named, Pete, he didn't want to be seen as a boss though. Of course, he was in charge, but he wanted the company to seen as a family. We were a family unit where everyone was equal, which I think was a brilliant way of thinking. After all, I was in the office 8.30am-5pm every single day, that's 37.5 hours a week where I'd be together with my work colleagues.

21

My boss used to arrange social activities too, from just a chit chat at the pub on a Friday, to a boules tournament where each of us worked in pairs to achieve top spot. We also did a presentation task which really took me out of my comfort zone. I walked our ofice dog, Teddy from time to time,
especially on a Friday lunch time when Sally, our
 receptionist was not in.

Once we did a Colour Run in Birmingham for Breast Cancer
 Now. See, the wife of my boss had Breast Cancer and he was spending a lot of money so she could receive treatment abroad. I think it's so wrong that this medication is not available on the NHS. I mean there are footballers on
 500,000 a month and they were having to pay hundreds for medical treatment.

Anyway, my boss travelled the world with his wife. He really made her life, the best it could before she passed away. It's such an honour to have worked with such a nice human being like my boss. He was so good to me whilst I was ill too, he made sure I was paid by using my holiday and sickness pay. Pete really cared for his employees, in fact I recently met up with Sally, the receptionist lady I used to talk to at VTUK. It was just like the old days when I met her, I was able to talk to her freely and really connected
with her.

One thing I didn't really enjoy at VTUK was the feeling o
 being trapped in the office every day. I hated having to be sat at my desk for that period of time. Yes, I enjoyed the work

22

I had to do but I wish I could have done it more, when I wanted to rather than within a number of hours. Time didn't drag at all, except when it was the last day before Christmas. I was so busy I hardly had time to chat.

Looking back, I had a multitude of jobs at VTUK from writing blogs, designing emails, social media, PDF e-guides to producing press releases. I was able to do these tasks whenever I wanted to. This is exactly how I want to conduct my work from now on. I want to work but on different projects. I spoke with my brother yesterday, we talked about work. He suggested that I should go freelance. I think this would be an amazing idea. I'd be able to work when I want to work. I'll have no pressure from a higher tier, only of course from the client but if I do the work, the pressure is nowhere to be seen.

Be kind to yourself

I'm thinking of going freelance, hence why I set up Design With Dan

I wake up every morning thinking that I should be working for a company but deep down I know I shouldn't. My Mum says, "now is the time to focus on yourself" and that's exactly what I'm doing. The media consistently pump into you that you should be working five days a week but for some people like me, that's not possible. I couldn't go out and work five days a week and not focus on myself as a person.

When I say focus on myself, I mean I'm focusing on my wellbeing. Focusing on how I feel day to day, how I'm generating meaning within my life. I'm tryign to eat healthier and exercise more. In other words, creating a HAPPY mindset for myself. A HAPPY mindset will allow me to develop a BELIEF mindset. I call it a 'belief' mindset because this is

23

exactly what it is. You develop a belief that you can do things, like start a new job, like learn new things, like start to drive.

It's this BELIEF mindset we all need, not a mindset where we are constantly worried about the next little thing. The media need to start marketing the idea that we can live a life alongside a working day. Work should be fun, it should be something you enjoy, it should be integrated into "you" as a person.

Writing on from this, I've decided to start my own business. This is a major accomplishment for me, I really feel I'm starting to get that BELIEF mindset back again. I'm calling it Design With Dan. I'll offer design and marketing services. I've bought a Mac (a computer, not a raincoat) and installed the Adobe creative suite on it. I can then start enhancing my skills in image manipulation and desktop publishing. I've always been interested in this side of things but have never had access to the software. Now I do and can start making the impossible, possible.

At the minute as I'm writing this goes by, it all seems like a bit of a dream. I know I can pull it off, I can have my own business. It's going to take time, I understand that. Anyway, I've set up the website for Design With Dan, it looks amazing, of course it's going to get continuous improvements. Follow my blog, website and social media to see if Design With Dan really does come true, that's designwithdan.co.uk by the way. I also have my blog livingwithdan.com, sorry for the short plug. At the minute with my social media, I'm feeling optimistic, my TikTok just hit 1,000 followers and is still growing. That's not all, I'm starting to broadcast live on TikTok with a number of guests.

If I had to rate my happiness from 1-10 today, I'd probably say 8, if I had to rate it when I was working full time, I'd say 6. Working doesn't allow you much free time which made me quite low. I felt dictated by the company to go to office at a certain time. They were nice and everything, it just felt like you were trapped work wise. Progress is key; it gives you meaning and with meaning, your life becomes meaningful. If you're working full time, yes you have money, a house, a car and all the material goods but are you HAPPY?

Your Personal Design & Marketing Service With Dan

Happiness is a notion I strongly encourage you to read up on. Money doesn't always make you happy. I've realised I don't need to work in a full-time job ever again. I have the skills to run my own business. Don't get me wrong, working for yourself isn't for everyone. You must have a lot of motivation and self-drive. You need to be able to get up every morning and work whilst avoid all distractions. I clearly have this quality as I'm always up at 7am, ready to create new ideas, write my book, learn Photoshop, etc. It's risky though, you need clients. This is the bit which scares me, I need clients to work for which are going to pay me and I'm relying on them to make an income. It's scary but I must think back to when I was working full time. I don't want that feeling of being trapped in an office job.

I look at my brother and see that he has an amazing full-time job. He's learnt the job all by himself, he's learnt to code, so why can't I learn to use Photoshop correctly? It's the same principle and then I can start working on my own business. To be honest, I have learnt Photoshop, it's just a few advanced skills I need to focus on.

You can learn anything, it's simply a matter of mindset

Another example is my Uncle Gary, he's always been good at using computers. I suppose my brother, Aaron, gets the talent from him and me, of course. Gary worked for HSBC, you know that great big skyscraper in Canary Wharf. I look up to him, he's done so well for himself. My uncle still works in coding but works closer to home now. I look at them both and see them as successful, but you must question whether they are, HAPPY?

Now if they're reading this, they probably would immediately say yes, I am happy. If you look deeper into their life journey, do they really like working 37.5 hours a week?

A lot of humans tend to have a comfort zone. I'd say Aaron and Gary, make their working life a comfort zone. They know they need to get up at a certain time, go to the office or work from home, but what if something disrupts their routine? Routine is central to our lives, I'm sure if you're reading this, you have a routine and you rely on the structure of it. When Covid hit it completely changed all our routines. Sadly, I didn't cope very well at all, it's dramatically changed my life.

Chapter 4
Should You Get A Tattoo?

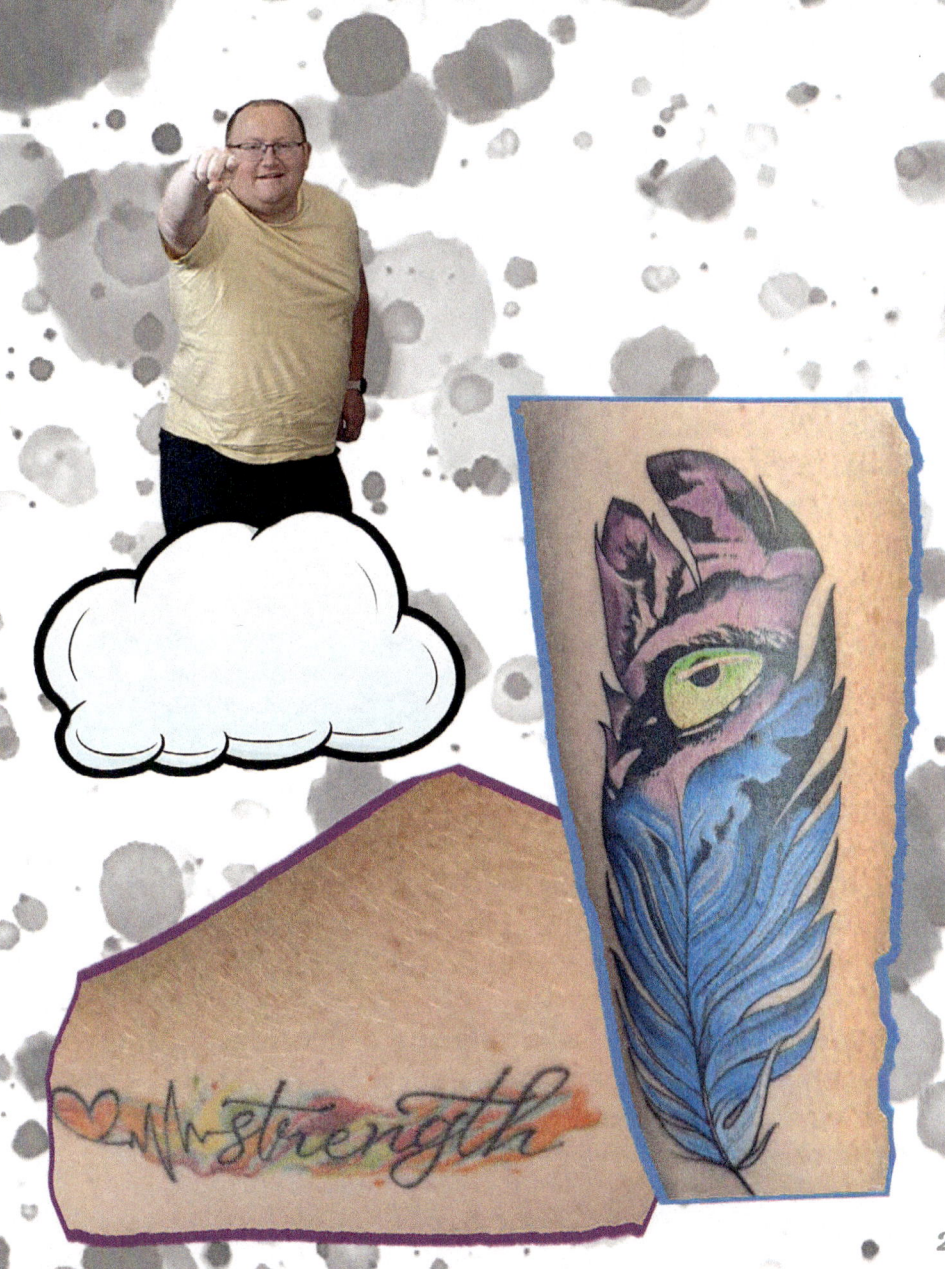

Ever wondered about the history of tattoos? I came across an article by the Welcome Collection, exploring the history of tattoos. The article explained that tattoos were originally used as a way of marking the skin of slaves. They were a common way of marking and identifying innocent people.

Today, tattoos seem to have much more of a mixed reception. HR News found that 30% of 25 to 39 year olds have at least one tattoo. They go on to explain that in the creative industry, tattoos were acceptable. The good news is that I work in the creative industry. As you know, I have tattoos, in fact I have 7 of them. However, in law, politics, or a form of accounting, tattoos were viewed in a negative light.

We're constantly told it's wrong to have a tattoo. We're told we should have clean skin, be healthy and smart. I'm sick of this so-called 'perfect culture' which we all have to adhere to. The amount of thin, glamorous models, you see in magazines. Whether they"re male or female, it's evident that we're supposed to look like them. Everyone is different, we're fat, lumpy, obese, spotted, freckled, nail bitten creatures, who all possess different unique talented skills and skin form.

I feel people with tattoos are often judged too much. Doesn't the saying go 'don't judge a book by its cover'. Many people are seen as ugly, if they're covered in tattoos. It's almost like tattoed people have something wrong with them,.

Being 'different' used to be seen as a negative. I mean the obvious example is the Hitler regime. Hitler promoted the idea that everyone should be white, not have a disability, tattoos were even frowned upon. This ultimately led to mass murder, jews, black people, autistics, they were all killed in concentration camps because they were all DIFFERENT..

D. I. F. F. E. R. E. N. T

Fast forward to the 21st century and the idea of being DIFFERENT is being celebrated. There's street parades for gay pride, even disabiliity pride. More countries are accepting same sex marriages and the idea of having a tattoo is becoming more convincing. This is an amazing thing of course, the idea of normality is becoming more and more blurred. This idea that we should have a perfect body, clean, natural skin and healthy lifestyles. It's all becoming mashed together to make everyone unique.

But with difference comes similarity. in other words, our heart tells us that we should be different to everyone else, but our brain counteracts that. The media tell us we should all be the same, that we should follow each other like a gang, hence with difference comes similarity.

Being different should be celebrated

Whether it be autism, ADHD or mental health, it's important not to label yourself too much. Yes, have a tattoo recognising your disability. Don't use your disability to avoid things though. You can do things; you just need that BELIEF mindset. Most importantly, this mindset will take time, it won't happen overnight. Work on your mindset and adapt it to suit your needs.

Don't use your disability to avoid things

What if you end up paralysed? Put in a wheelchair? Left to fend for yourself? This is exactly what happened to my Mum.. She had to learn to walk from scratch, after being paralysed. Today, my Mum can walk but sometimes if her emotions are triggered, her legs will wobble. Since then, she's got all sorts of tattoos with positive things to motivate her. This is typical example of how tattoos can help people, just like it has me and my Mum.

When I took my Mum to America, we were on the ferry coming back from the Statue of Liberty. My Mum's legs started wobbling. Loads of security guards came rushing to help her. The problem was, as humans our instinct is to go and help someone in that situation. She didn't need help though. The more help she got, the worse her legs get because she's thinking about what's happening. If she's left to focus on walking, her legs will behave 'normally'. I'm glad to say she got off the ferry okay. We even avoided having to pay the ridiculously expensive hospital fees in the USA.

When I got my first tattoo, I was extremely nervous. I was so scared I'd walk out halfway because of the pain. The decision to have the tattoo was quite easy really, I'm different, so I thought why not have a tattoo to stand out. Pain is such a topical thing,

If you can stand it, why not put yourself through it, to get the result you want. This comes back to my mum's journey, my mum is in extreme pain every single day. She wakes up in pain, works with pain and goes to bed with pain. I thought if my mum can resist pain, why don't I take on the pain myself. Plus, I had just recovered from a tongue operation, they thought I had cancer on my tongue.

On the day of my first tattoo, I remember my Mum taking me into the tattoo shop. It smelt of bleach and had fake needles and blood on the wall which didn't really reassure me. We arrived and met a man named Kane, my tattooist. Kane had all sorts of tattoos and piercings on him which instantly made me judge him as a druggie. Kane isn't a druggie, it's the depiction the media have put in my head of people with tattoos. Despite having tattoos, I knew Kane was a kind and friendly person and had something about him. Like I've said before, I don't judge, I always give a person a chance to be friends, no matter what they look like.

Be Kind

During the tattoo session, I told Kane my life story. He told me he had an 80-year-old who would come in to from time to time. That reassured me I was in capable hands. Before he put the first needle in, I was so nervous. I didn't really notice the painful burning sensation happening around me.

That's how I would describe the pain, it's like a burning sensation. It's nothing more than that, there's no real pain. I've always thought of tattoos in the past of being with big, hefty needles that go deep inside you. It's nothing like that. My first tattoo was of a Harry Potter Deathly

Hallows triangle with all four of the house colours within it. It looks amazing and still does to this day.

The second tattoo I had was one I'd been planning for a while. It's three puzzle pieces, the puzzle piece being a representation of autism. Now, the puzzle piece is a bit of a debatable subject when it comes to representing autism, I like to think of the puzzle piece as being an autistic symbol. It's something unique but fits in with society. I think it's a magical symbol and represents the autistic community. I'm like a puzzle piece as I'm unique, creative, funny and different. My tattoo has three puzzle pieces, they're all different in colour and display the words "live", "laugh" and "love" within them. Live your best life, laugh along the way and love everyone around you.

I had to think deeply about my third tattooa as it was going to be on my arm. It's the saying "strength" written in posh writing with a heartbeat. Every colour you can think of is behind the text. I see it every day and it really encourages me to keep going, even when things are tough. You wouldn't believe the number of times things have been difficult and I've looked at my tattoo. When I go to the gym and I'm on the treadmill, I keep reading the tattoo on my arm. it encourages me to keep going, even though it's so difficult to just get there.

Since having my psychotic episode, I've come on leaps and bounds. This hasn't been easy but ultimately this is the result of my inner strength.

When I was running, I had to keep telling myself I could do it and guess what, I did. In fact, if you've read my first book, you'll know that I ran the London Marathon and Bournemouth Marathon in 2019, that's a whopping 26.2 miles. This required so much mental strength, I must keep reminding myself of my amazing achievements.

wMy fourth tattoo was another Harry Potter one. I kept thinking how bare my previous Harry Potter tattoo looked. I wanted something to go with it. So I decided to have a bright blue Patronus tattoo attached to it. The tattoo is a beautiful deer to represent the blue
smoke coming out of Harry's wand when he casts the Patronus spell.

My next tattoo was going to be a feather with the picture of a leopard's eye. It looks so cool. Some might start be thinking to themselves, why I need to have a tattoo? Just because it looks cool and has a lot of detail, well the truth is I'm not just having it because it looks cool, I'm having it because it has a deeper meaning than that. For starters, the feather is a symbol of power and strength which coincides with my tattoo. The eye represents my eye, it's supposed to be always watching over
me whilst the blue to purple fade is amazing and makes the feather stand out, plus it's colour and colour is my thing.

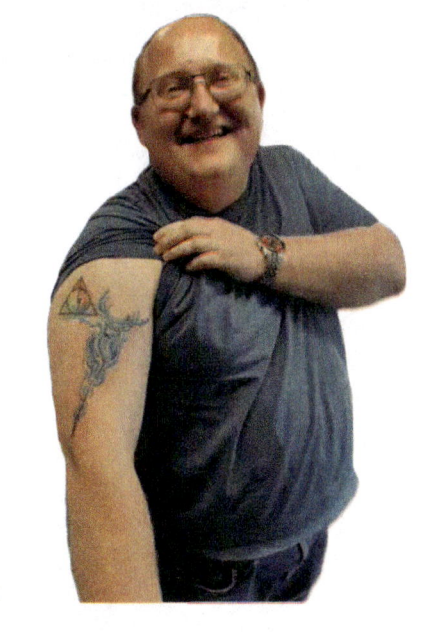

My favourite of all is my blue stitch, tattoo from the Disney film, Lilo & Stitch. I love it as the stitch looks so cute and the words "ohana means family" blends in with the vibrant stitch. Animation and Disney is a love of mine, so I think this works well tattooed on me. This was particularly painful as it was sort of under my armpit, at times I was clenching my feet to bare the pain. To say tattoos aren't painful is really an understatement, but if you can brace them, go ahead.

33

Chapter 5
Is It Normal To Be Lonely?

Friendships are so hard to have, especially if you are autistic. It's so hard to break the ice and connect with another person. Breaking the ice is so important for me, as it's gives me the acknowledgement that I can talk to that person. If I break the ice, water will run. In other words, I'll start to get more confident with that person.

I often lack the social skills to connect with indviduals. Finding the right words or a simple subject to talk about is so hard. Over my life I've been lucky to say I've had two or three friendships. In this book, I want to break them down and study what's given me joy within them.

I've recently been attending the Warneford Hospital to take part in therapy. We're exploring whether there's a link between loneliness and psychosis. Basically, we've been discussing my social life and social connections. When I say we, I mean myself and a therapist named Lorna. Lorna is a Scottish blonde lady, aged around 55. She's easy to talk to, like most therapist really. Don't judge me, but I prefer chatting to female therapists one to one, rather than male therapists, I just find them more calming. Saying that, I don't often come across many male therapists anyway.

After visiting the Warneford hospital for therapy, I realised I've carefully chosen my social groups and connections. We drew out my social map, which gave me a very clear outline of how I am socially connected within society.

35

I discovered that I'm happy about attending my art group and my peer support group, run by Oxfordshire Mind. I also have my gym sessions and organise a walking group.

Grab a piece of paper, write down the social groups you attend

What I got from therapy was the understanding that having a social connection is vital for our happiness. Human beings are social creatures, we learn from each other. We share what Nick Morgan calls "mirror neurons" which allows us to match each other's emotions "unconsciously" and "immediately". He explains how we as humans are "most comfortable when we are connected". Nick explains how, for an individual to achieve success they must develop a "sense of inhabit space and modify it in order to fulfil the role they want to achieve". Alright, this might be going a bit deep, but it does make sense. We as human beings must have a social connection, we simply cannot live alone, we must have a connection we can identify with to fulfil our way of life.

Whilst examining the importance of friendships, I feel I'm lacking close connections. I don't have another human being I can connect with on a close level. By closely, I mean, a girlfriend, someone I can have a meaningful conversation with when things get a bit tough but also embrace the good, hot weather.

UPDATE - I've found a **GIRLFRIEND**, she's called Amy and I love her so much.

The thing is, I hate touch, I hate it when I'm expected to cuddle or kiss someone at a party. It's not just having to cuddle with someone, it's knowing when to cuddle.

Nowadays, it's knowing whether it's acceptable to cuddle. For example, the situation when you leave a party, you have to hug with men and women. I'm okay with saying goodbye but the hugging and kissing, that's another story. I just tend to put my arms out when a lady tries to hug me. I'm kind of unsure on what to do. If a lady kisses me, I accept it but never kiss them back. It's this kind of autistic behaviour that makes me autistic. Social interaction is difficult for me, but I always push myself. The thing is, when it comes to embracing with people, there's all sorts of complications involved. You can be accused of sexual misconduct so easily, all it takes is a touch of a boob to put you in jail for 10 years. Yes, I struggle to establish relationships, whether that be online or in the real world. I tend to talk to someone and then move on. For example, when I go to my art or peer support group, I talk to people, but I just can't find the courage to expand my connections. For example, I could ask them to go for a coffee or go on a day out.

I want to ask my friends for a coffee (I don't even like coffee)

If only I could pluck up the courage to ask them. I guess we're talking comfort zones here, when it comes to comfort zones, you have three circles. The green circle, that's your comfort zone, the orange circle, that's your growth zone and the red circle, that's the panic zone, the zone you want to avoid.

The more I expand my social world, the more confident I'll feel. Last month I asked a friend of mine to go bowling, she said yes but ufortunately it was Mother's Day when we wanted to go.

Sometimes I just feel so alone

If I had to evaluate the meaningful friends in my life, I'd say I have three at the minute. They are Bea and Alex. Of course I have Amy but she's my girlfriend. Sadly, my close friends are starting to fizzle out again. I'm not talking on Snapchat to Bea as much, whilst Alex is very ill. I have my friends at Mind too, my friends I meet on a Wednesday and my family, I see these people in physical form on a weekly basis.

To me, my research at the Warneford Hospital was wrong. I don't think there's a link at all between loneliness and psychosis. I think there's a link between autism and psychosis. Not to worry you or anything, but mainly autistic people are lonely because they find it difficult to make friends. This could then lead them to depression which could then trigger psychosis. This is just a theory of mine and it's something I believe.

For me, friendships take a lot of determination, as well as connection. I must 'connect' with that person over a certain topic. For example, 'football' is a topic I talk about a lot, especially with male friends. The thing is, I only have so much I can talk about, so it's quite difficult for me. The thing is, I should look at the positive things I've done when connecting with others rather

Autism Psychosis

38

than looking down on my life. For starters, I have written two books about autism and mental health. I have design skills and I'm slowly developing it into a business. I have a blog which attracts hundreds of readers on a daily basis. I've ran two marathon including London and Bournemouth Marathon as well as 100 half marathons.

There's so much I can talk about to generate a friendship, it should be so easy for me. Getting into those situations is so hard for me. It's clear, people must be patient with me to develop a strong friendship.

Being autistic makes it so hard to make friends. Once you have a friend it feels so good though, just like it was when I met Amy. It feels enjoyable, like you have a soulmate. Just a quick Google, revealed several reasons why friends are a much needed part of your life:

- They benefit your health and wellbeing.
- They can help you in times of need.
- They can elevate your self-confidence.

I've got so many adventures to tell you

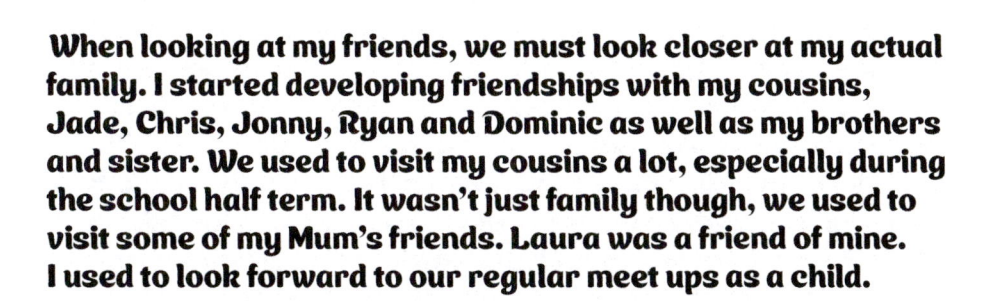

When looking at my friends, we must look closer at my actual family. I started developing friendships with my cousins, Jade, Chris, Jonny, Ryan and Dominic as well as my brothers and sister. We used to visit my cousins a lot, especially during the school half term. It wasn't just family though, we used to visit some of my Mum's friends. Laura was a friend of mine. I used to look forward to our regular meet ups as a child.

Apart from family, I've had a few friendships that have developed. From what I remember, the first friend of mine was a boy named Chris. We met at primary school. I can't remember how the friendship started but I do know it brought me much benefit to my health and wellbeing. For example, I used to invite Chris to my birthday sleepovers. Year after year I'd invite Chris to a sleepover where we'd watch a film and then open presents the following morning. I used to look forward to my birthday sleepovers. Chris also helped me in times of need. Chris helped me a lot during my secondary school days when I was bullied.

Secondary school was full of times of need as I was bullied a lot. Chris made sure he was there to talk too when I was struggling with the bullies. I suppose in a way he became a kind of therapist.
Chris also gave me confidence, we used to walk home from school together, travel and go to football, we even went to watch Oxford play at Aldershot. This gave me confidence to travel to football matches by myself. There's also been a few times where I've gone to London all by myself. This confidence has come from the leadership Chris gave me. If you've seen my TikTiok, you'll have spotted me travelling in London.

Going back to London, Chris taught me how to use the London Tube. When I go to London now, I'm very confident using the Tube. Travelling is a simple thing for me as I've done it many times. If you do something, over and over again, you get used to it. Breaking outside your comfort zone slowly becomes easier. As I said previosuly, I went along with Chris to Aldershot and we used the London Tube. Whilst travelling with Chris, mentally I was preparing my mind. I was telling myself what I needed to look at, which trains go where, etc. I store this information in my brain for a day when I need it most and I'm on my own.

The first time I went on the Tube, it was for a business meeting with Micro Rainbow International, a LGBTQ+ charity, I was volunteering. I remember Sebastian, the Director of Micro Rainbow, saying to me, "let's go for some lunch".

I thought we were just going to get a sandwich, but we ended up at an Italian restaurant. I was shy to begin with as I didn't want to choose something too expensive from the menu. I went for a simple cheese and tomato pizza to begin with, but I remember having a great big chocolate mousse for pudding. It was delicious and built up my confidence. As well as my business meeting in London, I've travelled by train to Birmingham to see Villa play football. I remember waiting for the train on the way back and a Manchester City fan ran onto the train tracks. I coped with it well though because I knew what to do, thanks to my friend, Chris. That was to keep back and let the police deal with situations like that.

Overall, Chris was an amazing friend. I still have precious memories, I'm sure we both treasure. My instinct is telling me to try and reconnect with Chris. The thing is, Chris has moved up north, so it is difficult to arrange a time for me to come up or him to come down.

Chris wasn't the only friend I've had in my lifetime. My second friend was a skinny, blonde, talkative chap named Robbie. Robbie was a kind, caring boy, he was a fan of playing Nintendo games like Zelda and Mario. I used to walk to school with him and all he used to go on about, was the games he was playing. It was an enjoyable conversation between him and me though as I'm kind of into gaming.

I remember me, my sister and brother used to play outside with Robbie. We used to go down to a supermarket with our bikes every Sunday at 4pm, when this supermarket was closed. We used to race each other around the car park and pretend we were doing Formula One. This is the kind of imagination we as kids used to have. We went exploring in the woods, pretending it was a den. To be honest with you, I enjoyed getting away from Robbie from time to time. He could get a little annoying. I apologies if you're reading this Robbie. I remember Robbie always knocking on our door, just as we were having tea. We used to ignore the door and he used to just go away. I had fun times with Robbie.

Chris and Robbie were my main friends throughout my childhood

Since my school days I've had a few friends, nothing has come close to the relationship I had with Chris and Robbie. During university, I had a close friend, or you could say colleague as we were studying together.

She was called Jackie; Jackie was from Uganda and had a completely different culture to me. We got on well and we made each other laugh, my relationship with Jackie could have led into a closer relationship. Her culture was completely different to mine though, that made me feel uncomfortable so it would have never worked out.

Then there was Toby, he was a nice chap. I met him during the disabled week, Coventry University organised before Freshers Week. We used to go to the comedy night together, we had plenty of laughs together. Toby was a confident person and really outgoing. Nowadays, I check his Facebook regularly to see what he's doing since leaving university. He's a representative for the disabled union and working in a high-level role. I actually just re-connected with him and we're planning on meeting up.

So, let's conclude, clearly a social connection are vital for our wellbeing, making them part of normality. We've seen this by looking back into the past and evaluating our meaning as human beings. We as humans need to connect to develop meaning in our lives. By connecting we eliminate loneliness and become happier.

My research at the Warneford Hospital with Lorna helped me see how selecting specific social groups are key to living your best life. Friends are part of normality and that is quite clear to see, nobody should be lonely.

Chapter 6
Do You Need To Drive?

Ah, the normalities of life, going to university, owning a house, paying the mortgage off by the time you're 70, driving a fast car across wide streches of tarmac. Just because you turn 17 doesn't mean you have to drive a car that could potentially kill. Nowadays, there's so much pressure on people to meet the "normalities" of society. Why do we need to learn to drive?

I don't know how people like Clarkson, Hammond and May do it. They drive all sorts of wacky vehicles and in foreign countries too. They all drive on the left hand side of the road too which makes things even more complex. it's madness, how on earth do they not get crushed by anxiety?

Learning to drive was like learning a whole new language for me. Being autistic certainly made it harder, but the thing is I did it. I'm so proud to be able to say that i can drive. When I first learnt to drive, I was lucky enough to have an amazing instructor named Colin. Colin didn't let me off the hook just becase I was autistic, he treated me like any learner driver. In fact, I drove back to my house on my first lesson, it was even across a dual carriageway. I remember my lesson vividly, my driving instructor pulled over and told me all about the car, from the gears to the clutch. Then he threw me in the drivers seat, well not literally and I drove for the rest of the lesson.

I'm so thankful for the way Colin taught me to drive. It has certainly made me into a better

45

driver today. Just putting me into the car and telling me to drive was scary but I did it. Obviously, he didn't force me to drive but there was still the pressure for me to learn. Today, kids avoid so much and blame it on anxiety. Yes there's anxiety but there's pushing yourself out your comfort zone as well. By the end of my first lesson, I had driven about 20 miles. It took me 40 lessons before I passed, just before my 18th birthday. Then I was kindly gifted Pass Plus by my driving instructor for my birthday, which was so nice of him. During my Pass Plus, we drove up to Coventry in the snow would you believe. I was scared, considering it was the first time I had driven on the motorway! I did it though, I pushed myself out of my comfort zone and really got used to driving on the motorway.

Now, I want to come back to the idea of anxiety, in particular, the anxiety I get when I drive my car. I worry about whether there's going to be anywhere to park when I get to my destination. I get anxious about whether I will have an accident, I get anxious over whether I will break down and have to call the RAC. The thing is, none of these things have happened to me for over five years. I need to put these worries to the back of my head and focus on the here and now. The present is so much more important, take notice of what's happening now rather than what could happen. There's no point in predicting the future, when the future hasn't happened.

My car broke down when I was on the way to work once. I ended up stuck in the outside lane. Luckily, another employee who works by me

stopped to help me. We noticed
a puncture from some glass in the road and tried putting in some special tyre liquid. That didn't work, so we called the RAC. They came out within 20 minutes which felt l like a lifetime. It's always worrying when you break down, you always worry that you'll never get home. Anyway, I made sure my car got a new tyre and I went on my way.

I suppose the rise in anxiety can be put down to the way we live our lives. We rush everywhere, expecting to be places in minutes. People expect to be at a destination without anything or anyone getting in their way. If one tractor turns up, they'll get stressed. The thing is, they're creating their own stress, there's no need to
get angry, enjoy the moment of going slow. Look around you, the sun is out, the day is beautiful.

Many drivers get in their vehicles and become a different person. We become violent, aggressive, miserable and could hurt a fellow driver or pedestrian. We as humans need to slow down and think about life in stages, rather than one clump of goodness.

Back in the old days, there were very little cars on the road. During the war (I sound like my grampy now), people used to walk or cycle to work. People are suffering with mental health as we're always on the move, we have no time to stop.

According to Jama Paediatrics, "20.5% of youth worldwide now struggle with anxiety symptoms", that's nearly doubled since the pandemic. That's not all, most of these are children. The NHS is struggling, nobody has any money and mental health is on the rise. Society needs to find ways of helping those going through a difficult time. Children are growing up with a poor mindset that doesn't teach them growth. Encourage your child to try new things whilst take on new opportunities, Children of today expect things to be put on a plate for them, rather than working towards their goals. This makes them more likely to experience anxiety as they aren't learning about new experiences.

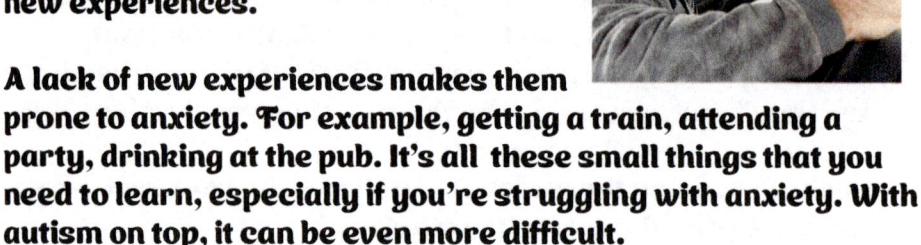

A lack of new experiences makes them prone to anxiety. For example, getting a train, attending a party, drinking at the pub. It's all these small things that you need to learn, especially if you're struggling with anxiety. With autism on top, it can be even more difficult.

Going back to questioning whether it's normal to drive, overcoming anxiety is vital. If you're getting in the driver's seat you need to make decisions quick and be competant. Driving is all about confidence, kids of today may struggle to drive if they don't have a huge amount.

If you have confidence, you can do anything

With more cars being driven on the road, driving is becoming harder
than ever. Our lives are busy, a restful, peaceful life is so hard to come by. Why can't we adapt to a more relaxed way of living? This is especially important if we want to save the planet as the o-zone layer is being destroyed. Why do we have to drive everywhere?

We drive to the shops,
to the cinema, to school and work.

People are terrible for driving places, when they should walk. For example they'll get in the car, just to go down to the local supermarket or to the local pub. One thing that isn't working is electric cars. They really need to do more research especially if we're going to get rid of petrol cars. I mean, who's going to wait an hour for a car to charge, when you can get petrol in 2 minutes. The advancement in batteries really needs to happen. It's something the government should be considering.

When it comes to electric cars, they really make it hard for people on the autistic spectrum. There's so much change for an autistic person to process. For example, the addition of an automatic handbrake. Being autistic and having OCD, I like to check whether the handbrake is on or off. It will make it so much harder for me if I have to use an automatic handbrake. Don't get me started on an automatic gearbox!

Saying that, I like to think that I can process change rather than accept I can't. This way I'm not stuck in the same hole forever. I've been doing a course called "One Step At A Time" with the charity, Mind. We learnt about comfort zones. Basically, as I mentioned earlier in the book, there's three types of comfort zones, your comfort zone, growth zone and panic zone.

Coping with change is hard for me as an autistic person. I need to focus on staying in the growth zone for as long as I can. Think of the growth zone like an elastic band, you can stretch them, stretch them as far as you want.
Don't stretch them too much as they'll snap and you'll end up in the panic zone.

Growth Zone · Comfort Zone · Panic Zone

Chapter 7
Should You Have Children?

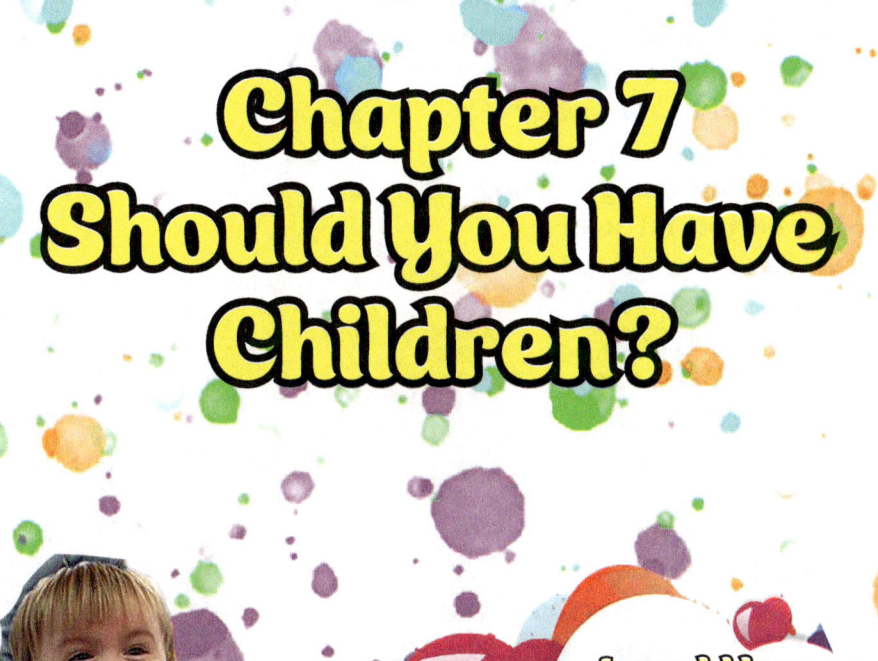

I would love to leave somebody behind

I love my niece, Millie. She's nearly 3 now, would you believe? Every time I go around my sister's house, Millie is there shouting "Dan" and she greets me with a loveable smile. Sometimes she can go all shy and her bottom lip goes and she starts crying. She does this with a lot of men especially strangers. I think she finds them intimidating. On the other end of the spectrum, females are happy, friendly people, who tend to greet you with a smile. I kind of get this feeling too. I'd much rather talk to a female than a male as they come across much kinder. Of course, Millie can identify with the females too.

I don't think Millie will struggle in terms of her education. She can count to 12 already, she knows everything, about everyone and has such a cute smile. Back to the case of me having children. I recently met an amazing, cute, happy, adventurous, beautiful, smiling, cute girl named Amy. Can you believe I've never kissed a girl in my life? Yes, never, until last month. It was the most incredible, amazing feeling ever. I'm in tears of joy at the moment. We know it's certainly possible for us to have a child in the future. After believeing I'll never have a child, my dream has certainly come true whilst most importantly I've met the most amazing person.

Millie is as special to me as her mother is, a.k.a my sister. Being autistic, sometimes I feel I should have been the one producing the first baby, but no, it's not always you, the eldest. Why is it always assumed that the eldest child will produce children first?

To look closer at normality, we must look back in time. A lot of the pressure to produce a family comes from war times. Children were expected of you. Nowadays, there's not so much pressure on you to create a family, especially if you have autism or struggle in social situations.

Family means everything to me

I'm looking forward to meeting my brother's daughter, Holly and be Uncle Dan, again. Kayleigh has now had Holly, she's gorgeous, she has big bright blue eyes and is so alert. The first time I went to see her I was rather nervous, as I had to drive on my own. I had to drive my car and park somewhere I had never been. I met Holly and bought her a cow which makes a mooing sound when you press its arm. I held Holly for an incredible 30 minutes. I even managed to make Holly hold my finger whilst she slept.

"OHANA MEANS FAMILY."

My brother had the cricket on when I visited his house. When it comes to sport, football and darts are my number one choice. Cricket is slow and boring and really doesn't appeal to me. I enjoy playing cricket occasionally with a tennis ball though. That's part of my autism, it hurts when balls hit me at pace, like a hard cricket ball.

I did play football at my brother's stag do though. I remember being fouled by Kayleigh's Dad playing football. It did hurt but I got up like a stereotypical man would and moved on. I'm not very good at football to be honest, my balance is terrible. Once again this is down to my autism, I struggle with steps especially going down them, I often take one step at a time, if I don't, I'll feel like I'm going to fall over.

Anyway, going back to my niece, Holly, I held her for 30 minutes whilst watching the cricket at Aaron's house. That was my first visit, on my second visit their dog Lola was there. Lola is being trained to walk around Holly and not attack her. Although Lola is a dog, she might be feeling left out so it's important to remember to include her,. Sadly, Lola has now moved out and loving life, living with some experts Beagle trainers.

Good news, my sister has just had another baby, her name is Sophia. I visited her the other day, she's so cute and cuddle. She's a whopper, 8 pounds 7 ounces in fact. I have three special nieces now, every one of them means so much to me, I treat them as my children, I love them so, so much.

Deep down, I know that Millie, Holly and now new born, Sophia will look after me as I get older. My siblings may not be around to look after me after all. Going back to the question, "whether or not it's normal to have children", the evidence in this paragraph clearly shows, creating a family is a form of normality, it's simply evolution.

The thing is nowadays with our busy lives and hectic schedule, having children can simply be too much. It can have a dire effect on our mental health. Putting myself in my sister's shoes, she must look after Millie and Sophia now, it's equivalent to a full-time contract, the amount of work you have to do.

Millie, Holly & Sophia Are My World

When it comes to having children, acceptance is a huge thing. It's like when we grieve for someone who's died, we need to accept that they have now gone. One good autistic trait of mine is accepting death or accepting a decision. For example, the time I had a car accident. My car was a write off, I didn't know what to do. I had no car and my only option was to get a hire car. I accepted that my car had gone, I accepted that I was going to have to take on a huge challenge of claiming on the insurance. I accepted that I was working from home the next day.

Having a family, is all about acceptance. As a couple, you need to agree with each other to have a child. When you start trying, you need to agree on a name as well as where it's going to school. Together you must decide what clothes it's going to wear, how it's disciplined, what treats it gets. There's so many things you need to agree on as parents. Normality and children, it's just a decision that needs to be made, some say yes, some say no.

Chapter 8
Want A Mortgage?

Everyone needs a roof over their head. I hate walking down the street and all you see are homeless people. I remember when I was doing a run back in 2019, all we saw were homeless people living in London, it's so sad to see. Yes, there are foodbanks which really help those in need but surely as a nation we can do more.

The normality that we all should own a house is disgusting from my point of view. We really need to treat those living in extreme poverty with a bit of respect.

As I said above, I visited London for a run in 2019. It was for one of my half marathons I was going to take on. Unfortunately, the run got cancelled because of the wind. We had a good time though, we looked around the Olympic Park and had something to eat instead, don't tell anyone but I preferred that to running 13.1 miles.

I should think myself lucky that I have a roof over my head. The house I'm living in at the minute is a four bed and is big enough for what we need. We have a huge garden, plenty of space to relax and enjoy life. I still live with my Mum but I'm independent in my own way. I have my own car, my own money, I pay my way and I'm my own person.

It's not common to find people still living with their parents nowadays, especially as we live through the cost of living crisis. Seeing the state of people not being able to afford their own homes is horrible. This the harsh reality of living in a capitalist society.

People are struggling to survive, the cost of living is at an all-time high and things are getting ridiculously expensive. Look at the Prime Minister, he and his wife are worth £730 million pounds! I couldn't think about having that sort of money. If I had that sort of money, I'd buy a big house where we both could live, sorry that's a lyric from Elton's 'Your Song'. I'd buy a house with a swimming pool and bowling alley. in fact, I could spend a whole day bowling. I'd buy a normal car but with all the gadgets, I don't want a big flashy car. Of course I'd buy loads of chocolate to snack on.

I was going to buy my own house but after getting ill, I've decided not to. I'm not working, my savings are going down, so I'm going to concentrate on getting myself better. At the minute, I'm going to the gym, attending my Mind peer support and art group whilst I'm also doing an Adobe InDesign and Photoshop course. Having my own house is now a dream rather than a reality. It's simply too expensive, I can't afford to pay a huge amount of money each month on the mortgage.

Owning my own home is now a dream rather than reality

I used to dream of owning a house, but the thing is, it's so expensive. I used to dream of having gadgets in my house, a giant 100 inch TV, security cameras, a PlayStation and maybe even a pool table. The thing is once we own something, it costs more and more. It's the upkeep of keeping that item, like a car for example.

I watched a TikTok explaining how we live in constant capitalist world. We're trapped in a cycle where we get a house, car, mobile and are constantly having to pay for it. isn't this the normality of society? We're constantly being fed information, that we should have the latest mobile, car or gadget whilst we're stuck in a mundane job that we rely on to survive. What I want in my life from now on is time to do things that make me better whilst working. The work I do should be enjoyable, fun and full of achievement. This is why I'm setting up my own business. I'm calling it, Design with Dan. This will allow me to work when I want to work, rather than be contracted to work certain hours. Of course, I'm still looking for a part time position to go alongside my business. If you haven't come across my business, search designwithdan.co.uk and you'll find me. My website is so cool, it's all about me and how I can work with you to design or market your business. I've always wanted my own way of making my own money.

Moving back onto houses and the normality of owning your own home, my sister and brother both own houses and they're both doing well. When I say well, I mean they're surviving the cost of living crisis, they both have a roof over their head and are enjoying life.

My sister's house is amazing, due to the fact she has her husband, Jack to do the DIY. Jack's good at DIY, that's why he works in dishwasher repairs, he's even come round to my house to fit flooring! My sister's house is perfect, although now they have Millie and Sophia to think about, they need to start contemplating moving house. My sister's house has an incredible

59

garden, would you believe it used to be a muddy field? Now it has grass, a shed and
decking on it. Mind you, Jack spends half his time cleaning the decking as Millie often drops sandwich crumbs on the floor.

My brother and my sister-in-law's house is just as amazing as my sisters, they too have just enough room to enjoy life. They have the perfect place to look and nurture baby Holly, they have a beautiful living room with a sofa, PC, PS5. My brother even has his own office to do his work in, as he works from home everyday.

With my brother and sister both owning a home, I kind of feel a little bit left out. The thing is, I don't have a mortgage hanging above my head. Yes, it's nice to have a place you can call home but paying for it is something else. Of course, there's more to life than money but having the commitment of getting up for work everyday, it's so draining. I really think it should be law for people to work four days a week, five is far too long especially when you think how many hours people work anyway. Owning a home, being dictated to in today's capitalist society, I'll give it a miss…

I dream of maybe, one day living in a home I own

Chapter 9
We're All Going On A Summer Holiday

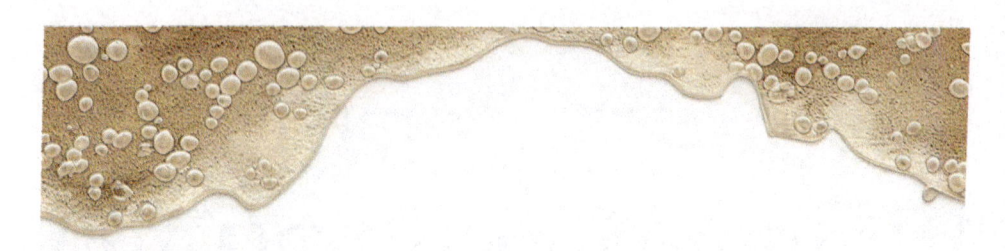

There's so many people who don't go on holiday! I've always assumed that it's normal to go away every year. I was at Mind last week and one of the facilitators asked whether anyone had seen the sea? I couldn't believe my eyes when people hadn't. Sometimes I take my life for granted, I assume everyone else has the same life as me. There are so many challenges people go through.
I couldn't tell you how heart breaking it is for me to here that people will die, without ever seeing the sea. That's the horrible thing about capitalism, if you have money, you can do what you want. if you don't, you end up stuck in a room all day.

I recently watched the film, I-Daniel Blake. The film depicts a man living in poverty. He makes friends with a mum of two boys and from there, their relationship blossoms. The film is so hard hitting but the true message comes down to love and happiness. It's so important to have these two important things in our life. We don't need anything else.

Love and happiness is such a strong emotion. When I watch those romantic films and see a couple walking across the beach, smiling at each other. They go on adventures with each other, love each other until the day they die, this is my dream. I dream to find a women.

Good news! I have found the women of my dreams, her name is Amy and is the most amazing person you'll ever meet. I met Amy online and then we met in person and we just seemed to click. It's like we've known each other for years. She has cute glasses, beautiful eyes, long black hair and is the nicest person ever. Just for all my readers, here'e a pic of me and Amy together. Plus, we're both autistic which makes our relationship even more magic. If you ever, ever think to yourself that you can't do something, I urge you to please, please keep believeing. Dreams do come true, just like they are with me.

To put it bluntly, I've been on 3 holidays this year. I know that's a bit dramatic! You only get one life and I'm making the most out of mine. If you've read my previous book, you'll know how much I love holidays. I have so many treasured memories from my holiday adventures. I just love the feeling of letting your hair down and escaping away.

My first holiday this year was to Butlins in Skegness. I went with my family, it was a fun and exciting time, especially seeing Millie dancing. If you recall, Millie is my 3 year old niece who's really starting to grow up now. I love watching her dancing and enjoying herself, she really loves music and gets into it. She's such a happy girl and I wish a lot of people were like her. The only person I know who's like her, is me really. I'm happy and cheery and I'm starting to find the confidence to get on that dance floor.

If you've been to Butlins before, you'll know it can get busy. Finding a table at the club was a nightmare as pretty much 80% of the seats had gone. The busy atmosphere stressed me out a lot. That's first world problems though after all I'm on holiday, I've seen the sea and I'm enjoying myself with my family.

I remember when I decided to take Millie to see a show by myself. It was early in the morning and my sister and brother-in-law were getting dressed. I thought I'd help by getting Millie out of their hair. it felt like a great deal of responsibility, taking care of Millie. At first, I parked the pushchair near the stage and me and Millie watched the show. Millie went quite shy at first, especially around other children. She often goes shy when there's new people about. I'm shy at first but once you get to know me, I'm confident and talkative. I'm such a funny and nice guy to be around.

The next place on the cruise was New York. We saw some amazing buildings including the Empire State Buildings, the Rockefeller Centre and Times Square. Seeing them as we were sailing into New York was like something else, it really was a dream come true. New York comes alive at night, we saw a giant dressed up gorilla, spiderman and other characters. My cruise was simply incredible and will be a holiday I'll remember for the rest of my life.

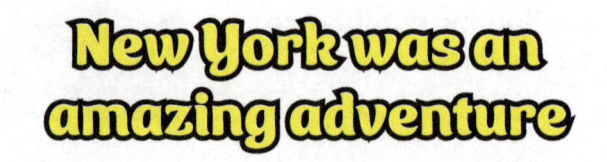

New York was an amazing adventure

My third holiday was to Mallorca where we went for a whopping 10 days.
This was another amazing adventure as we went as a family, me, my mum and brother.
Often I don't enjoy sitting out in the sun, it just feels a little tedious. I always get scared I'm going to burn which doesn't help. Mallorca did involve some sunbathing but we balanced it out with activities. Ultimately, I enjoyed our days in Mallorca especially the Aquagym and Water Polo.

I'm so glad I got the confidence to do Aquagym in the pool. It was very hot in Mallorca but dancing in such a warm, lovely, cool environment was relaxing in a way. Dancing is such an anxiety provoking activity, my brother struggled to get up and dance, but I did it. To be honest, I don't enjoy dancing as it's difficult to think about the moves. Aquagym was a bit of fun though, there was no pressure. All we had to do was have a good time with each other. It was first thing in the morning so it was good to get our bodies moving too.

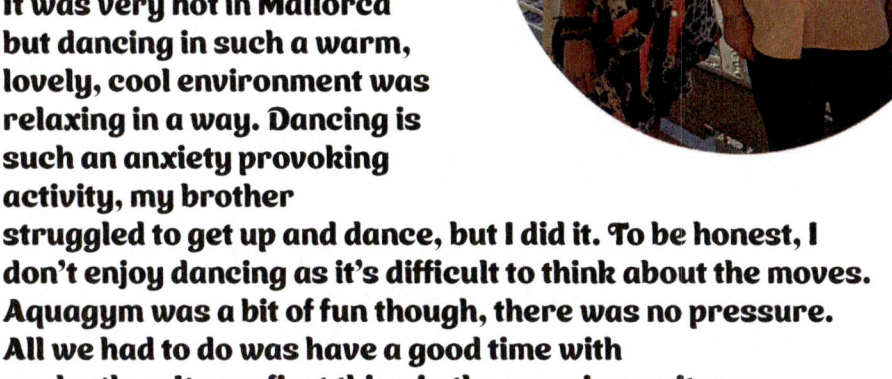

The time you spend with those you love is so precious

Chapter 10
My Family Support

'Ohana Means Family'

I've always had someone to communicate with. I see it as normal to belong to a large family, after all my family is huge. I feel sorry for those people who live alone and have no one. I mean I could have no family, I could have no money and I could be struggling. I do have family though and that's the amazing thing about my life.

If I had no family, I suppose I'd try to seek out friends in my life. Going to social groups like the gym, art classes and gaming groups would help me build a social life. It's hard as socialising is tricky for me. I see my autism as a unique way of perceiving the world although it is the main reason for my difficulties.

Let's look further into uniqueness, more specifically into the idea of how we as humans perceive things. I was talking to my Art Teacher about the idea of normality, we agreed that normality often takes place within us, as individuals. Each of us perceives a standard set of normalities, For example, I perceive my brothers and sister to be who I think they are. In the next couple of paragraphs, I'm going to describe all my family and explain the way I perceive their normality.

I have four siblings in total, each having their own unique way of thinking. They all behave differently, they all have their own way of confirming to society. First we have Charlotte, she's my sister, you probably guessed that. Charlotte has black hair she's slightly on the chubby side (STOP – hang on, I say she's chubby, but does she think she's chubby? Maybe being chubby is her way of being normal).

Me and Charlotte love our food, just the other day we went to KFC with Millie, my niece.

Then there's Aaron, he's my brother, you probably guessed that too, Aaron is the handsome one, he has my grampy's looks about him. He's slightly tanned, tall, has dark hair, you can think me later Aaron (STOP – Aaron is handsome because I've been told by the media that being good looking is skinny, tanned and muscular, but does everyone perceive this normality? It's a complex question, but not everyone would find Aaron attractive so surely our normality comes down to our individuality?). Believe it or not, Aaron has a very similar attitude to me, he'll go out, work hard and get to where he wants to be. Aaron works in IT doing HTML with websites and stuff.

That's the three of us, Daniel (that's me of course), Charlotte and Aaron. Now my Mum re-married, so I have two other siblings. Thomas and Harry have a different Dad, but that doesn't make them any different. The first of these siblings is Thomas, Thomas loves his video games, just like I do. He goes to a special school but that doesn't make him less likely to get a well-paid job in the future, it's just his brains slower (STOP – Thomas doesn't have a slow brain. Thomas just works in a different way to others making him bette.)

We are all DIFFERENT
We are all UNIQUE
We are all SPECIAL

Let's go back to the conversation I had with my art teacher about normality. Now my art teacher is dyslexic, making him neurodivergent just like me.

We disccussed about autism and chatted about how we are all different and skilled in our own way. My art teacher explained that he was good at seeing things in 3D, whilst I struggle a bit with that kind of thing.

Going back to my siblings, lastly, we have the baby of the pack, Harry. Harry is clever, but he seems too afraid to show it. Harry struggles attending school due to his anxiety. If he was attending school much more, I really think he could go far (STOP - Getting out and challenging yourself is key to living a happy life. Does going to school really help us? I know it's important but we learn things everyday without even going to school.). Harry's a talented soul, I just sometimes wish he had my confidence.

Family is something I can't see myself losing. I've lived with my mum, dad, brothers and sister all my life, that's 32 years of support. I think it's evident that each of us have a unique way of perceiving normality, My use of the word STOP, really highlighted my way of perceiving my siblings. My sister, Charlotte is chubby, Aaron is handsome, Thomas is slow and Harry is talented. That's sounds a bit harsh, but it's something I needed to do. Normality is a very harsh and judgemental subject. We all individually have different ways of percieving each other.

One thing that's a complex subject is my mum and her mum and dad. In other words, my Nanny and

Grampy Shutford. My mum and her brothers and sisters have all fallen out with my nan. They haven't talked to her for almost 20 years. They treat her and my grampy as if they're dead, which I think is harsh. I wouldn't dream of doing that. Would you ever stop contact with your mum or dad? I'm not taking anyone's side but when you address this situation with the issue of normality, it's clear this is not a normal situation.

We as humans are told we need love, family and support. That's not all, my Uncle Robert completely ignored me for most of my younger years. I didn't get a card, birthday or Christmas present. I can't understand why he ignored me? It's just now, within the last five years or so that he's come into my life. If he were to read this, he would feel quite guilty. I mean I don't hate him because of it, it's just a bit confusing. If we were to put this into the context of me and my nieces, Millie, Holly, & Sophia, I would never ignore them. One reason could have been because he was diving around the world. I mean my Uncle Gary travels a lot. Gary's been to South Africa, Japan, Germany, he was even front page of The Sun after England won 5-1 against Germany in the World Cup. He even used to travel to London everyday to work in that giant HSBC tower in Canary Wharf and still sees me regualrly.

I understand as you get older, you drift away from family and I appreciate that but you don't ignore people. Family is your tribe, they look after you in times of need, when you need them. I think the message is clear, never leave them, no matter how hard times may be.

As you know I'm autistic, so I don't hold grudges against people. I always think it's
important to care for people and most importantly, FORGIVE. If you judge someone by their appearance, it's very stubborn of you. People with this attitude struggle to see the talent in everyone. For example, my brother, Aaron is super talented at coding and writing HTML

whilst my sister is talented at producing prints. I see how they both can help me with my design business. That's Design with Dan which I was talking about. When I first got ill, I would have never thought I'd go through some of the things i did. I saw clowns, I woke up at my sister's house screaming that God had cured my autism. I actually believed that God had cured my disability.

My family were there to support me throughout my psychotic episode. Whilst I was in hospital, my Mum brought me up her chocolate pudding which I loved. My sister delivered me some of her delicious, chocolate cake pops. If you don't know what cake pops are, they're cakes with chocolate over the top! Family are so crucial to your wellbeing, especially whilst going through such a difficult time. I think the support they gave me whilst being in hospital proves how important they are.

Forgiving your family is so important, I believe that having them or a close person as support is crucial for your mental wellbeing. The support they provided me throughout my psychotic episode was amazing. Forgiveness is such a special ability, it's the ability to put the past behind you
and move on.

Forgiveness is such a powerful skill

Chapter 11 Should We All Exercise?

Exercise is important, not just for our mental health but for our physical wellbeing. Exercise and eating healthy, it's the key to happiness, but is it really? If you had to ask most people, they'd say they don't exercise. They'd say they stay at home or work most of the day. There's so much they could be doing though, whether it's walking, running, gym sessions, squash or even tennis.

My mum is always going on about losing weight, about how she looks, about how she feels so much better being skinny. The thing is, she's so obsessed with her personal image that she doesn't have time to enjoy life. I remember when we were in Mallorca and I was taking pictures on my phone of her. She always wanted to see how she looked before I uploaded it to social media. Does it matter how you look? It's just a photo, a special memory. When she's a pile of ashes, the memories will dissapear, so don't be embarrassed about one single photo. My brother was exactly the same, we ended up having an argument about the photos I posted.

It's so hard in the modern world we live in, with Just Eat and Uber Eats on your doorstep. It's so easy to pick up your mobile and order a takeaway, you don't even have to speak to anyone. I need to cut down on the number of takeaways I have. It's ridiculous, but I just seem to eat anything I pick up or in fact see.

If you read my last book, "Living With Aspergers: Daniel's Story", you'll know I love food, in particular

73

takeaways. There's a whole chapter where I explain about each takeaway. I know I'm overweight, I know I'm fat, I know I'm obese. I'm just one of 80 million people around the world who are obese. I just like to blame it on my metabolism, as I've lost weight in the past.

We are all going to die eventually, so why not enjoy eating chocolate? Enjoy the experience because once we are dead, we won't have the ability to taste. The only memories left will be the ones are family and friends remember. Sorry to be so morbid, but it's the truth and the sooner we as people recognise that, the better. Enjoy life, enjoy the experience, make the most of every single minute of every day because once it's gone, it's gone. Life is such a precious gift; does it really mean having to exercise and put yourself through pain? Does this really have to be what we call "normality"?

The number of slim men and women you see, the media are telling us that we should be like them. I'd rather not fit in a child's size t-shirt. As a nation, we're becoming like the US; the UK is obese and it's down to the wrong food being eaten and the lack of exercise being done. The thing is, how do we know it's the wrong foods? The media likes to create a kind of moral panic amongst society. I mean the number of doubts the media put into our mind. is it healthy to drink tap water? Are we eating red meat too often? Is dark chocolate good for you? All these rumours make us as humans worry, our alert system goes from 1 to 100 in seconds. We're bred to sense danger, that's why negative news is much more appealing to us than positive news. Moral panics are littered in the paper, they are there to give people a sense of anxiety.

Anxiety is the key word here, if we didn't have anxiety, we wouldn't care what we looked like, about our health or how long we live. I remember my grampy, he was such an amazing person, but he always used to worry about the future. His worry was a good thing though as he is no longer with us and my Nan is fully supported. He always used to save a lot of money and had a good job which secured their futures. The thing is, that worry could be the reason he is no longer with us. Of course I can't blame it fully on worry, but it gave him a deep sense of anxiety. I really feel that we could be living longer if we didn't have the pressures of having to fit into society. The pressure of running a household, having a family, losing weight and being healthy.

I used to do a lot of running. In my first book, there's a lot of running advice that will really get you motivated. What I want to do in this book is look at why I started running? To run long distances, you need a certain mindset, a get up and go mindset. A mindset that you can switch on and concentrate for hours. A mindset that is determined to reach a goal, to reach new limits.

Exercise is brutal if you think about it, your heart pounds so quick you struggle for breath. Of course there's simple exercises, like walking but real elite athletes must come close to dying if they want to achieve. Exercise is the ability to push yourself to the brink, push yourself to death. With that comes fear, what if I die? What if I collapse? What if I simply can't do it? When we talk about motivation, there's motivating yourself to simply get up. This kind of motivation is completely different to an elite's perception of motivation. It's the ability to say to yourself, this is risky, this could kill me, but I've got to do it to achieve success.

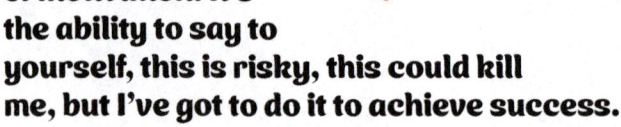

I have so much admiration for elite athletes, they've pushed themselves so hard. I used to blackout after going on the cross trainer, my eyesight would completely go. It's so scary. if I do lose my eyesight, I'll quickly grab a glass of water and my eyesight will come back. I'll always have a soft spot for running. I still get the same feelings from it but I simply can't run for long. I'll be at risk of triggering my psychotic symptoms and damaging my mental wellbeing.

When it comes to exercising, the good news is that I've now signed up to Pure Gym. In fact, I've just hit 50 visits to the gym. The gym itself is a bit intimidating as you walk in. You have to scan your mobile before entering a kind of pod like thing. Now if you're claustrophobic you won't like entering the pod but you can do it. Perhaps you could enter via the disabled doors, if you suffer from claustrophobia? Once you're in, the only thing I didn't like was having to use a padlock to lock my stuff away.

I mean how easy is it to install some kind of key mechanics rather than having to use a padlock. I always worry that my stuff will get locked in the locker as some of them are a bit dodgy. This anxiety is easing though as I'm going more often to the gym.

I've just hit 50 visits to the gym

The first gym class I attended was a spin class. This is where you sit on a bike and pedal as fast as you can. Have you ever tried cycling for 30 minutes? It's tough and it eats into your energy. Everyone comes out the spin class looking like they're soaked. It's good fun though, although it feels so tough when you're cycling.

The gym is friendly

I'm glad to say I still attend Pure Gym, but I go to the bodytone class. That's right, I'm working on my figure, I want to tone up my body so you can see all my beautiful muscles. Only joking, I just enjoy the class, it's small, friendly, enjoyable and everyone is really kind to each other, no matter of their ability.

I remember when we used to do physical education in school. Some pupils used to bully me when I was exercising. It was mainly verbal abuse I had to suffer. People would make fun of me whilst I was getting dressed in the changing room. I ended up hating PE.

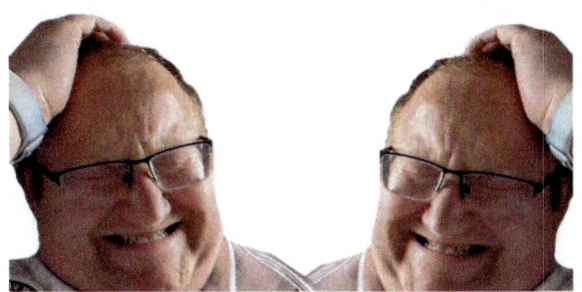

Since then, I've ran two marathons and 10 half marathons. I have a great love of physical exercise. Back in school, I hated physical exercise, it was so emotionally draining as I was bullied. I was overweight which made it even harder for me. I also hated the time limit you had when it came to getting dressed and then attending the next lesson. As I'm autistic, I often struggle getting dressed. I just need a bit more time to do things. Anyway, nowadays exercise and me, they kind of go hand in hand.

Moving on, the relationship between exercise and technology is interesting. I know you're reading this thinking, what on earth has tech got to do with running? My answer is everything. Technology is invading the exercise sector, think smart watches, think interactive exercise bikes just like Peloton, think interactive treadmills. I saw one years ago at the Gadget Show Live, I'll be astonished if they haven't developed since.

Nowadays, footballers wear vests which monitors heartrate, their touches on the ball, distance ran, all sorts of data. Then you get video games. When I was younger there was the Wii Fit board, where you could stand on it and exercise. Then there are games like Ring Fit where players have do squats whilst holding a weighted ring. The digitalisation of exercise is encouraging a younger generation to be active. More needs to be done to encourage youngsters and middle aged humans to exercise. Tech has certainly helped me on a daily basis. I count my steps, moniter my water intake and use my watch at the gym.

Chapter 12
Be Connected, It's Normal?

Facebook, Instagram to TikTok, the world has gone digital. We live in a digital world where everyone can be found anywhere. Whatever you want to know about me, it's out there in the digital world. For my career, this is a good thing. I want my work, whether it be images or videos to be seen. I must be social, as I'm a social media guru, I have to know the ins and outs of the digital landscape. Like, how to manipulate consumers online so they buy the product you're selling.

As an expert in social media, I know businesses want their product to sell. Money isn't the most important thing, they want your DATA. I can't express how important data is. Data allows companies to target users specifically on their tastes.

In the next chapter or so, you'll hear about my gambling addiction. When I was gambling, you could see I had been by the amount of gambling adverts across my Facebook feed. Multiple gambling websites were advertising across my social media, all telling me to come and gamble. My search terms within Google were all gambling related too, making it even easier for me to gamble.

Another thing to consider is the use of cash. I use my card for everything rather than cash. I know I shouldn't as cash is starting to become extinct. I mean, there are even venues now completely banning cash payments, how can they even do this? Cash used to be a significant part of our lives. When we use our card, it's being used as a way of tracking our spending, our location or spending habits.

This data is starting to be shared so businesses can target you. I can't say for sure if this is the case but I'm very concerned that it might be. We as humans are starting to be exploited, our personal data is at risk of being stolen and sold. As I say, data is big business, you can sell data for a lot of money if you come across it.

How are people meant to cope with these digital changes? The normality of using a mobile is being accepted into society but it's not normal for elderly people. They're having to adapt to what I call the 'new normal'. Imagine being born in the 1950s? The war has just ended, you grew up washing yourself in a tin bath. TVs were just coming onto the scene, you listened to just the radio or read newspapers.

Elderly people seem to only understand 'simple' things. A computer is another world to them. I've often thought of starting computer lessons to help enrich those without computer skills. It's not just elderly humans who struggle, it's those who can't afford tech in the first place. Several people at my peer support group don't even know how to use a computer. A car park in my local town only allows you to pay via mobile now, the London tube is cashless. Facebook is also seen as the norm, if you're not on Facebook, you don't really exist.

Tech can create so much anxiety, even if you DO know what you're doing. I think it's important for the youngsters of today to become connected online. It's vital children understand how to use tech in the world we live in. I kind of feel

sorry for the elderly or those with limited
knowledge of mobiles and tech. They're kind of being left out.
I recently signed up to an SEO (Search Engine Optimisation) course. It made me realise
how we can create media based on what people are searching for. By manipulating content through keywords, companies can specifically target you as a person.

This form of manipulation and consumer marketing is so beneficial. If you ever wanted to set up a website and business, you can and get a lot of website traffic, quite quickly. Having this knowledge of the web not only allows you to understand how it works but gives you the ability to work in SEO.

It's so important to understand the digital world we live in

Anyway, is it normal to be connected? The evidence above clearly shows that you can look at the question from two angles. It's normal for you to be connected if you're already connected. You understand the technology behind it and the way it works. On the other hand, if you're elderly or live on a low income, you're less likely to use mobiles or a computer, making connectivity almost impossible. Normality comes through your values and your individuality, if you believe it's right to be connected, that's your normality. if you don't have the knowledge of using tech, the normality of connectivity will more than likely NOT exist. Face to face communication will be your norm.

Chapter 13
Are We Overwhelmed?

Are you overwhelmed? The point I want to address is, 'What's the normality of people being busy? We're constantly being consumed by articles, images and videos. On the road, people are as angry as ever. If you wait a second at a roundabout, you'll more than likely be told off by the driver behind. They'll beep angrily on their horn, vigorously waiting for you to speed up.

People are constantly in a rush, there isn't a minute to stop and just sit down. People are being consumed by advertising. Everyone wants the next "new" thing. Why can't we just slow down and take a break? After all, a busy lifestyle is no good for our mental health. There's 24 hours in a day, that's 1,440 minutes, 864,000 seconds for you to fill. All we do is RUSH around watching videos, movies, playing the latest game, getting the latest gadget, driving as fast as you can to the next destination and getting so frustrated if you must WAIT.

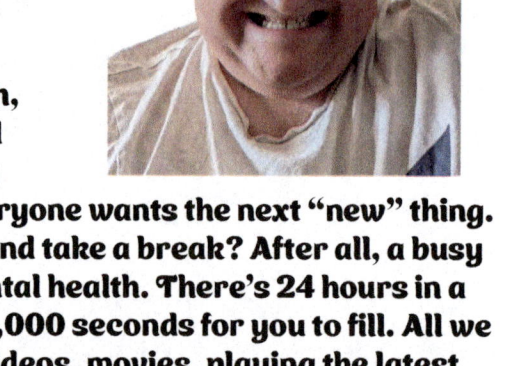

We're constantly being bombarded by this notion that we always have to be doing something. You never see an advert on the TV advertising the idea of doing nothing. I have a t-shirt that says it's okay to just breath, in fact, doing nothing is a relaxing way of putting your mind to rest. I tend to be on the go all the time, always wanting to do an activity. Whether it's working on my blog or business, SEO or videos. Then there's housework, building LEGO, diamond art or simply watching TV.

I realise that life is for living, make the most of every single second of every single day because when we die, we die and that's the end.

I'm a great believer in making the most out of life. Of course, it's important to sit down and recognise the here and now. It will only enhance your wellbeing. When it comes to doing nothing, try sitting on a chair with your feet flat on the floor. Make sure you're in a comfortable position, then breath in and out, slowly. Think about what you can hear or smell, open your eyes and have a look. What's on the table beside you? What can you smell in the air? You can even imagine your safe space, like a beach for example. Alternatively, think of a flower and a candle, smell the flower, what does it smell of? Then slowly blow the candle you're thinking of, only slowly so the flame flickers. That's an amazing way to de-stress and meditate.

People are always in a rush to 'consume' the next thing. They have no time to focus on the mediative side of life. If you're like this I'd recommend small forms of meditation, just to allow yourself to calm down. I'm not saying you can't go about your day with a busy attitude. What is important is getting stressed over little things. When I worked for Top Kids Accessories for 6 months, I continually got stressed over my Amazon listings. A lot of the listings wouldn't work and the spreadsheets kept failing when I uploaded them. I tried each and every day, but they simply didn't work. That's not all, more and more hair items were being placed on my desk for me to list. It was becoming overwhelming and I felt trapped which led to suicidal thoughts.

On the complete opposite side of spectrum, back when I was psychotic, I was manic. I remember playing Just Dance, dancing around the living room. It was a strange feeling looking back, I had so much energy and was really confident. It was like I was a completely different person. The chemical imbalance in the brain is incredible really, looking back at my psychosis it's unbelivable how you can suddenly become this completely different person.

Depression or mania, they are both difficult things to experience

There's clearly different perceptions of what people call 'normality'. We as humans, see different views of reality depending on how it's presented. This allows us to make judgements and decide who defines us. Nowadays, the media seem to promote our busy lifestyle.

Interestingly, back in 2020 the idea of going shopping completely vanished. The media responded to this and started advertising the idea of togetherness. The feeling of community came across much more than consumer products. In 2020 when covid hit, we needed to keep spirits high so people were encouraged to support the NHS, whilst help out elderly neighbours.

Is being overwhelmed normal? Studies suggest more and more people are becoming anxious. As humans, maybe we need to recognise when we need to STOP?

Chapter 14
Addiction Is Simply Normality?

TRIGGER WARNING
Reference to mental health, such as addiction

Gambling, booze, drugs, sex, video games, exercise to spending. Addiction is something everyone has to deal with at some stage. Some addictions are more harmful than others, but the fact is addiction is on the rise. There's no doubt addiction is a mental health condition.
When you get addicted to something you become engrossed in that activity and 'struggle' to STOP.
Within my life, I've had a few addictions, gambling being the main one. There is a fine line between addiction and an obsession. Of course, autism makes be vulnerable to being obsessed with something. My running past is a great example of this.

I want to open up about my troubles with addiction. I've accepted I have an addictive personality. My first addiction, well you could say it was more of an obsession, was running. In fact, I used to run three times a week back in 2019, this included a 13.1 mile run every week. I used to push myself to the limit to be the best runner I could be. I remember going for a run once on an icy day, I nearly slipped and fell down a hill into a car.

If you're addicted, I urge you to seek help

A lot of people wouldn't class running as addictive, they would say it's more of an obsession. It's not as dangerous as gambling or drugs but it can cause you harm. I think the running I was doing caused my psychosis to a certain degree. If you've got an addictive personality, which I believe most of us do, it's hard to open up about it.

As you can see, I feel quite comfortable to reveal my addictive nature as it helps me. Sadly, GAMBLING was another one of my addictions. Say the word GAMBLING out loud, say it over and over again. It makes you feel uncomfortable, doesn't it? When you GAMBLE you feel an excitement, a kind of rush going through your body. It's as if you're unstoppable, you feel as if you can do anything. You want it more and more and more, until suddenly you realise it's gone too far, you're ADDICTED.

G.A.M.B.L.I.N.G

When I first started gambling I used to have a £10 bet on the football a week. £10 was it, until I started playing what the casino calls 'free games'. I had a go on Sky Bet's Super 6 and predicted the football scores. You have to predict 6 scores and if you got them right, you'd win £250,000. Then came other 'free games', these involved picking bubbles to get a 'free bet' or 'spin'. I also played Sky Bet's 'spin to win' which gave you the chance to win 50p, a 'free bet' or 'free spins'. It started as casual fun with very little money involved until the 'free' offers vanished. I started using my money. 'Free' offers are there for a purpose, they're there to tempt you into using money. When you're on about 10 different gambling sites it can tot up a lot. I started depositing £20 a

week, £30 every day, £100 every day. I'm thinking to myself, "I'm winning, gambling is making me money". Woah, hang on a minute...

Gambling is meant to be FUN, it's an activity done for FUN. It's always within what you can afford. I see myself as a person who likes to make a lot of money. GAMBLING can be a dangerous business for me. I have plenty of the old dosh, I'm not afraid to admit that. I still have plenty of dosh to this day. Looking back, I remember making £1,000 on roulette, then losing it again 30 minutes later. I used to deposit about £100 a day, that's £700 a week, that's £2,800 A MONTH!

Suddenly, it hit home, I can't control myself. I'm gambling in my bedroom all the time. It makes no difference if I alter the deposit limit or use the gambling tools on offer. I simply can't stop depositing money, the bookie's are winning. I can't STOP.

The National Gambling Helpline
0808 8020 133

How do you STOP? The answer, BAN yourself. There's online tools such as GAMSTOP which will block your access to gambling. Online is key because that's where it's so addictive. Online, no one can say to you "I think you've spent enough now". I'm pleased to say I don't gamble online anymore. I still gamble in-person but only when I go to bingo with my family. That's no so secretive. I'm one of the survivors of GAMBLING addiction. I feel there are millions of young teenagers in grave danger. Due to peer pressure, it becomes simply impossible to STOP. I was on the bus the other day and these teenagers were talking about betting, I felt like going over and saying "BAN yourself".

It's as simple as saying to someone
"I GAMBLE"

My sister and dad both have a gambling addiction, my sister has banned herself but my dad continues to gamble. He says that he restricts himself, but I really think he'd be better off banning himself completely. Peer pressure has once again got to my dad, his friends from work gamble and it's something he feels he needs to do. He needs to gamble to fit in with his friends.

I hope I've helped someone writing this. I've opened up about my problems, why don't you? A lot of people, especially if they're young, are afraid to admit to themselves that they've got a problem. Now I'm 32, I've realised reflecting on the past and planning for the future is essential. It allows you to make sense of the world around you, especially if you're autistic.

I'm writing this as we're just about to go into 2024. I have a vision for next year, I'm going to be volunteering at Banburyshire Advic

Centre, managing their social media. I'm going to build a lot of Lego too. I've already bought myself a 4,000 piece Gringotts Bank, that's the bank from Harry Potter. Aside from volunteering, I'm also going to be writing this book, which is due out in summer 2024. I'm going to continue attending my art and peer support groups too.

Stopping gambling is hard, it's everywhere, especially if you're into football. Gambling companies are on footy shirts, advertising boards, TV and radio adverts. As a gambler, I know how easy it is to join a gambling site, you simply enter your email and away you go. There's a petition going around calling to 'end gambling advertising and sponsorship in football'. It currently has 124,778 signatures and it's growing. I urge you to sign it. Gambling is a problem; someone needs to fix the industry.

Today, it's exposing the younger generation to a potentially life changing addiction. This could result in mental health difficulties or even, I hate to say it, suicide. Addiction is common, it's a form of normality we tend to hide about ourselves. It's mainly because we're scared of being judged. Judgement is a stigma that we as humans should avoid. It's such a one sided way of seeing the world.

SEX addiction is judged on a huge scale. It's so wrong that people are victimised just because their addicted. SEX, it's addictive, that feeling just feels so good. That feeling that you're in love or just the feeling of being aroused. It's just one of many addictions people can face in today's world.

Chapter 15
What's Normality?

Just what actually is 'normality'?

It's pretty difficult to answer this question with a simple 'yes' or 'no'. Whether it's mental health, going to work, children, being connected or driving, we have so many ways of viewing normality. Think about the "Wizard of Oz"? Dorothy gets blown away in a storm to the Emerald City. She meets the scarecrow, the tin man and the lion. When she finally meets the Great Oz, his booming, loud, scary interpretation of himself turns out to be false. He reveals himself to be a tiny little old man. The Wizard Of Oz clearly shows how we can easily interpret things to be bigger than they actually are. Take for example, my business, Design With Dan, it's just me. I have no clients and make no money. I have a full-blown website which is being optimised by myself using SEO, The posts I do on social media make me seem a big business with multiple departments, when really, it's just myself.

The way we perceive things makes such a difference to how we live our lives. It works exactly the same to how we perceive people. I could judge a human for siting on a bench, smoking a fag with tattoos all over them. My brain instantly labels them as drunk or druggie. That's just the way I'm perceiving things, it's my individual perception of human life.

At the end of the day, tattoed people who smoke have a bad reputation.

94

As I explained in the first chapter of this book. A 'normal' person is often seen as someone who has a job, house, children, married, can drive, has a degree, no tattoos and is happy. The normality of today is completely different.

Within this book, we explored how mental health is becoming the norm. We addressed how covid could have been a significant factor in the rise of mental health cases. It's clear that whoever you are, mental health can impact you. Just look at me, I work in social media, have plenty of money and I'm an author but I still can have psychosis.

I also addressed the issue of work. I argued that the work culture of today is becoming more casual. Ever since the introduction of 'working from home', as a nation we're relaxing with work. This is a good thing, freelance work is beginning to rise. For example, I'm looking at ways I can make money without leaving the house. There's no need to leave home to make a living anymore. That's especially true if you work in IT, marketing or design.

Then I turned my attention to the rise of tattoos. I explained that tattoos are becoming more prominent in our culture. More humans want to share their story and inspirations in the form of tattoos.

People want to share stories in tattoos

Tattoos were initially seen as a way of marking slaves. Nowadays, tattoos are seen as something that makes you unique. One thing I realised whilst writing this book was how important social connections were. We need someone to communicate with, it's vital for our wellbeing. As I found out at the Warneford

Hospital, if we don't have a social side, we become lonely. If we're lonely, it makes it incredibly hard to start a family.

As humans, it's bred into us that we must start a family of our own. If you struggle socially, this becomes an uphill task. Connecting in the real world is one thing but connecting online is another. This is where my expertise comes in as I see myself as an expert when it comes to social media. I'm currently doing an SEO course too, that's about how to rank website's higher in Google. I'm aware many humans don't know 'how to' or 'do not' have access to the web, therefore we shouldn'ta ssume we are all connected.

Our everyday life is full of so many things which is becoming normality. The rise of social media has transformed how we consume media.

People can get online so easily now, gambling companies are finding it easier than ever to exploit audiences. Whether it be gambling, drink, drugs, video gaming or sex, people are becoming addicted to lethal activities, that could ruin lives in the long run.

I think we as humans need to look at our lives and see every human as a blank canvas. Don't judge humans by what they are doing or how they are behaving. Judge them on what they talk to you about. Who do they do for work? What family do they have? How is their wellbeing? Have they suffered from addiction?
What's normal?

Every human has a unique story

We are all
D.I.F.F.E.R.E.N.T

Let's Celebrate...

Find Me On:
X
Instagram
Facebook
TikTok
YouTube
livingwithdan.com

Printed in Great Britain
by Amazon